Another Castle

By N64Josh

Life lessons illustrated from Super Mario Bros.

This book is dedicated to family, friends, and NPC Fam, and especially my wife, kids, and parents who loved me through my darkest times.

Chapter 1: The Adventure Begins	3
Chapter 2: Nintendo's Adventure	13
Chapter 3: Mario's Adventure	21
Chapter 4: Enjoy The Journey	25
Chapter 5: The Side Hustle	35
Chapter 6: Mushrooms and Fire Flowers.	53
Chapter 7: Another Castle	57
Chapter 8: Only Moving Forward	63
Chapter 9: Hitting Reset	67
Chapter 10: Player 2	72
Chapter 11: The Final Boss	75

Chapter 1: The Adventure Begins

    This adventure begins in a time of candy cigarettes and bubble gum cigars. The year was 1986, and I was five years old. I would sneak out of church, cross a busy street and use whatever change I could find to buy said candy from a small gas station. I wouldn't use any quarters I found though, because those were reserved for a magical place known as the arcade. Every visit to the mall consisted of me dragging my dad past the toy stores and ice-cream shops to the only location that mattered, Aladdin's Castle! I can still see the red-tiled pillars being painted by neon lights as we approached, the faint sounds of bleeps and bloops with occasional "body blow, body blow" from the announcer of Punch-Out. I knew this place was magical because time would speed up while I was there. It didn't matter how long I was there, it was never enough. This was the one place I could be whatever I wanted to be, and the price of admission was only twenty-five cents. Saving the planet from aliens in my spacecraft, shooting robbers with a light gun, or becoming a warrior and taking on hordes of goblins. No matter what, I was in control of the adventure. The draw for me was that I could interact with the media and create my story within these games.
    I had watched hours of Transformers and the occasional HE-MAN (if my mom didn't catch me).

My mom, like many moms in the 80's, was told that if your kids watched cartoons with magic and played with toys from those shows that it would put them on a dark path. I always assumed that the magic cartoons could turn me into a wizard, and because of that I would go out of my way to watch. But no matter how many times I tried I was never able to cast a spell. None of my friends that were on the "dark path" from watching the shows could cast spells either, so in the end, all I missed out on were the half-hour commercials to get me to buy toys. For me, any spells that were going to be cast had to be in the arcade, if I could sneak a quarter into Gauntlet without my parents seeing me.

    Honestly, I was drawn more to the games where I could pilot spaceships, always looking for the chance to go on my own space adventure like Luke Skywalker. Flying a vector drawn X-wing through the trench of the Death Star was a dream come true. Fortunately for me "The Force" didn't fall into the magic category in The 80's Moms Handbook of Unproved Magic, so Star Wars was ok. Shooting lightning from your fingers was fine, but you better not cast a healing spell (I know you are reading this mom, and I am glad we can laugh about this now.) Since Star Wars games were on the approved list, I didn't have to watch my back while playing. Pac-Man, Popeye and Donkey Kong were also on the approved list. While gobbling up power pellets to eat ghosts or chowing down on spinach to save Olive Oyl was fine, it turned out that the red overall wearing Jumpman would eventually change the face of gaming. He also would take me on many adventures both on and off the screen.

    Jumpman, who would come to be known as Mario, was all over the television. Those half hour Transformer commercials had Nintendo commercials sprinkled in, and I wanted a Nintendo so bad! The urge to "Play With Power" had become strong within me. In the Summer of 87, I met Mario's friend Link and had the opportunity to play the Nintendo Entertainment System for the first time. I was finally playing a console that had two buttons! I'm not sure how many times I was told to go play outside, and I didn't care… I was finally Playing With Power! The "outside world" would always be there, but the chance to play Nintendo wouldn't last, so I ignored the demands as long as possible. I remember seeing the gold cart for the first time, and watching in amazement as the title screen flashed on with so many colors. This was like having an arcade at home, and I savored every moment. Unfortunately for Link, he didn't make the approved list, so we never were able to finish that adventure. Eventually, I was kicked back outside, but I had gotten the bug, and thankfully my aunt noticed.

Christmas morning of 1987 was going as planned, as the standard Transformer and Star Wars toys were under the tree, and all was good. I didn't even ask my parents for the NES because I knew it wouldn't happen, and I was okay with it. I was more than content with my action figures. Christmas was always a four-part ritual. Part one was Christmas Eve with my mom's dad and stepmom. I was always guaranteed to get some kind of clothing that would have got me killed on the playground had I worn it to school. Part two was getting my parents out of bed at an ungodly hour to open gifts unless Christmas fell on a day my dad worked on the farm. If that was the case we had to wait until almost 10 am to open presents, which to a 5-year-old was brutal. There were years that I wasn't sure if I'd make it because part two was usually the action figures and their vehicles that you hoped Santa would bring. Part three was my mom's sister, her husband and my grandma and they often showed up carrying large boxes. Part four was my dad's side of the family, where it was less about the gifts and more about the time together. Uncles, aunts, and cousins made part four the perfect way to end Christmas, but let's "be kind and rewind" a bit to part three and those large boxes.

I remember looking out the window at ten or eleven AM Christmas morning and seeing bags of gifts and one unusually large box. As the gifts were unloaded I made my way to the pile to scope out the name tags, the large box said "to the family," so I quickly wrote it off. We all finished opening our gifts, and then they had my sisters and I sit down on the couch together. The large box was placed on our laps, and we opened it. I remember slowly removing paper and seeing the gray Zapper. I couldn't believe my eyes. I was expecting a board game that I would never play. My sisters almost immediately went back to their Barbies, but I stared in wonder at its beauty. The Nintendo Entertainment System Action Set with Super Mario Brothers and Duck Hunt. This was my first gaming console, and I couldn't wait to get it hooked up. I had to wait for my dad to help me and he wouldn't help me until we had eaten Christmas lunch. I don't think any meal had ever taken so long in the history of all meals. Didn't he understand that there was a princess to save and ducks to hunt? With it finally set up I pressed the power button selected Super Mario Bros and started the game. Then I proceeded to walk right into the first Goomba and die. I started again this time jumping on the Goomba, and I felt like I got little extra out that jump by throwing my arms up each time Mario bounded into the air. Not gonna lie breaking that habit took some time. By that evening I couldn't even get past world 1-2, and I was getting frustrated.

At this point, part four of Christmas had begun, and there were family members all over the living room that my new Nintendo resided in. My uncle and I sat down criss-cross applesauce style and started to play. This is the guy that initiated and help feed my gaming addiction with frequent trips to the arcade or Saturday afternoon gaming sessions on the Atari 2600. He was 19 at the time and he was flying through these levels unlocking new worlds, and I couldn't get past 1-2. I fought back the tears. I was so angry because I wanted to save the princess, and I was stuck in the second level. He could tell I was frustrated and told me something that still echoes in my mind thirty years later, "enjoy the journey." I didn't want to hear it then, and at times I don't like hearing it now, but it was essential, and I will cover it later on. Christmas 1987 would be the day that spawned so many great memories from my childhood.

    My dad wasn't much into Super Mario Bros, but he loved sports games, and all sports games made it on my moms approved list. "No fighting games" was something I heard regularly, thankfully she didn't consider Mike Tyson's Punch-Out a fighting game (I am just as confused about this as you are). Sports games were the compromise that brought my dad and I together. I was super competitive, and it was during games of Double Dribble that he had to teach me not to be a sore loser. I would get mad that I lost and he would make me turn it off. I eventually put two and two together and "enjoyed the journey." It was with that same game that he taught me not to be a sore winner by making me turn it off if I began to gloat. Neither of us really liked basketball, but we would regularly rent Double Dribble. Our favorite football game was Tecmo Bowl. Bo Jackson, sweep right was the best play in the game, as you could run back and forth from end zone to end zone and never be touched. There were nights that he would take me to work on the farm with him, and we wouldn't get done until after midnight. When we got home, we would pour a big bowl of salsa and take turns making our way through the fighters in Punch-Out. As silly as it may sound it's one of my fondest memories. I saw the way my friend's dads treated them, and I knew that this was a rare thing. He would have had every right to be too tired, but he put being tired second to spending time with me, and it means the world to me to this day. I hope that I've been able to do the same for my kids, that they could have moments of knowing they are the most important thing right now.

    My mom didn't do much playing, but my best memories are of her cooking dinner on cold fall evenings with windows veiled in steam. Those were peaceful times, times when there were no cares in the world, for me at least. She cooked with sounds of Super Mario Brothers being played in the background and to this day that theme song takes her back to a time where her kids were young, to treasured times.

In 1989, with thirteen inches of snow on the ground, my little brother was born. We have a video of him coming home, and you know what song you hear in the background? Super Mario Brothers. Like I said my mom didn't play much other than Tetris or a game we borrowed called Gyrus, but she would listen to me go on and on about Nintendo this or Nintendo that. She couldn't have cared less, but she never let on, because it was important to me, and I was important to her. So she would let me tell her of all the adventures the plumber and I had gone on. I appreciated that.

I was obsessed with anything Nintendo, and I was only allowed to play for forty-five minutes a day and not at all on Sundays. I think this rule was also part of that 80's moms handbook. Nintendo cereal was a must, any Nintendo cartoon shows were a must, anything Nintendo was a must. In second grade a kid moved in who loved Nintendo almost as much as I did and we had different games! His name was Erick, and we quickly became best friends. I don't think I ever let him play as Mario and he still liked me. When Super Mario Bros 2 was released, he got to play it first, and the first thing he told was that Luigi's name had changed to Loogie. I, in turn, told everyone I knew and, well, looked like an idiot. We were young, so I really didn't care. All that we cared about was the sequel to our favorite game was coming out! He was my 'player two' for many years. I remember late night gaming sessions with Contra, just him and I taking on the hordes of aliens with nothing but the glow of the tv illuminating our small faces. That game had to be played at his house because it was definitely not on the approved list at mine. Sadly we grew apart through the years, and in 2000 he passed away in a car accident. I will always cherish the memories, but I would love the chance to hit that select button and have my first 'player two' back for one more game.

    My uncle and I have been gaming together ever since I can remember, but we spent more time with Mario in his later years on SNES and Nintendo 64. The same is true for my wife. When we were dating we played countless hours of Mario Kart 64, and Goldeneye. Nintendo has been a part of my life for almost the entirety of it and often is a common bond shared with friends and family. For me, it's not only the stories we play, but it's also the stories we create from playing together. What has always looked like a waste of time to some people, has been the best time spent for me. Most of the time it's not the experience in the game, it's the experience shared with someone close. I couldn't tell you how far my dad and I made it in Punch-Out that night, but I'll never forget the night. When I see

Mario, I see a lifetime of fond memories playing with people I love. As a kid, I wanted to work in games, but had no idea how to make it happen. It took me almost 30 years to follow my passion and begin the adventure towards working in the gaming industry.

It's been my side hustle now for over five years, and the journey has been a crazy one. I've met amazing people, been able to speak at a convention, and cover events that include E3 and PAX. My journey is still unfolding, my Princess is still in another castle. But through this book, I want to share what I've learned from life, and what we can glean from a 30-year-old game about an Italian plumber. Before we do, let us take a look at where Mario came from, and what it took to get him into our living rooms in the mid-1980s.

Chapter 2: Nintendo's Adventure

In 1987 Nintendo had become a household name but let's stop and rewind almost one hundred years prior. Nintendo was founded by Fusajiro Yamauchi who began manufacturing Hanafuda Cards, which were playing cards used for a variety of games. These cards were handmade and grew in popularity very quickly. The name Nintendo loosely translates to "leave luck to heaven," and luck often found its way to Nintendo. Roman philosopher Seneca once said "Luck is what happens when preparation meets opportunity," and this was the case for Nintendo time and time again. In 1791 a game called Mekuri Karuta became so popular and was so commonly used for gambling that it was banned. Many other card games were developed and banned, over the next few decades. Eventually, the government began to relax, and Hanafuda Cards came into being. There were no numbers on these cards, only pictures, so it limited the amount of gambling possible. Card games had become less popular due to the government ban, but Yamauchi saw an opportunity and began selling hand-crafted cards painted on mulberry tree bark. It was not an instant success, but eventually, the Yakuza began using Hanafuda cards in their gambling parlors, which helped the card games gain popularity once again.

Hiroshi Yamauchi took over the company at the age of twenty-one in 1949 after the passing of his grandfather Sekiryo Yamauchi. In 1953 Nintendo was the first company in Japan to produce plastic playing cards. Six years later Nintendo struck up a deal with Disney to sell cards with Disney characters on them. They sold the cards with a book which explained all the different games that children could play with them. This allowed the cards to be sold in Japanese households and it is estimated that they sold a least 600,000 in a single year. Because of this success, Yamauchi took the company public in 1962.

With the new found success of the company, Nintendo began venturing out into new business ideas. Most of these ventures ended up being failures. A taxi company, "love" hotels with hourly rates, instant rice, and Chiritorie vacuum cleaners. Toy manufacturing was one area where there was some success, but things were not looking good. Playing cards had reached a saturation point, and Nintendo's stock dropped from 900 Yen to 60 Yen. In 1970 a maintenance worker by the name of Gunpei Yokoi would eventually help turn Nintendo's luck around.

The year was 1970 and Nintendo was drowning in debt. Things were looking pretty dire until one day Hiroshi Yamauchi was touring one of the Hanafuda factories and noticed Gunpei Yokoi playing with an extending arm he made.

That extending arm would come to be known as the "Ultra Hand" and would sell over a million units. Gunpei quickly went from maintenance worker to product development. His engineering background was now being used to make electronic toys for Nintendo. "Ultra Machine" was a pitching machine that launched softballs that could be hit with a bat. It sold over a million units. The Love Tester could test your love, you grab one sensor and have your partner do the same and the machine would determine your love score from 1-100. Most of these toys can be seen in games like Animal Crossing, and some have made cameos in The Legend of Zelda and Metroid. Nintendo Beam Gun was another one Gunpei's inventions, and it would be the first light gun available for home use.

Nintendo began testing the waters of video games in 1972 with the Magnavox Odyssey. The light gun accessory Gunpei invented was used for the game Shooting Gallery and was manufactured by Nintendo. In 1974 Nintendo acquired the rights to distribute the Magnavox Odyssey in Japan. After the success of the Odyssey in Japan, Nintendo began developing video games for both arcades and home use. Color TV 6 and Color TV 15 were the first home consoles from Nintendo made in joint development with Mitsubishi Electric. These consoles were Pong clones offering multiple versions of Pong. Pong is basically table tennis where each player controls a paddle, and you score points when your opponent misses the ball.

In those days arcades were on the rise, and Nintendo wasn't going to miss the boat. Taito's Space Invaders was a massive success, and it spawned many clones including Nintendo's own Space Fever. Shigeru Miyamoto's first game was Radar Scope. It was a mix of Space Invaders and Galaxian, and it gained popularity for a short time in Japan. During that time the president of the newly founded Nintendo of America (NOA), Minoru Arakawa, ordered a large number of machines to be shipped to the United States. By the time the order arrived, the hype for the game had died, and Nintendo of America was left with thousands of arcade cabinets collecting dust.

Yamauchi wanted all hands on deck for creating a new game that could run on the Radar Scope's hardware. Shigeru Miyamoto pitched Donkey Kong, stating he had drawn inspiration from Beauty and the Beast, King Kong and Popeye. Under the supervision of Gunpei Yokoi, he began to work on the game. Initially, the game was going to be a Popeye game, but Nintendo failed to acquire the rights. Sticking with the love triangle idea that had been formed between Popeye, Olive Oyl, and Bluto, it became an Ape, a girl and a carpenter first named Mr. Video, and later Jumpman. The girl would come to be known as Pauline, named after the wife of Nintendo's warehouse manager, Don James. Jumpman was named after the grumpy landlord of the warehouse, Mario Segale who was trying to collect past due rent. Donkey Kong wasn't your typical arcade game. It had cutscenes to move the plot, heck it had a plot. Mario's pet ape fell in love with his girl and Mario had to rescue her. This game also offered more than one stage, in fact, it had four. Nintendo of America's staff didn't believe the game would succeed, but it ended up being a massive success in Japan and the US both commercially and critically. Nintendo licensed the game to Coleco to make a home version for numerous platforms. Donkey Kong, Mario, and Pauline were everywhere including cereal boxes and cartoon shows. Mario was voiced by Peter Cullen, who later voiced Optimus Prime in Transformers. Nintendo's stubborn ape was making them millions, but a much larger stubborn ape was about to see them in court.

Universal Studios filed a law suit against Nintendo in June of 1982 for trademark infringement of King Kong. Coleco and other third parties had buckled under the pressure from Universal to pay 3% of all Donkey Kong royalties. Nintendo, however, did not buckle and ended up beating Universal at their own game. Universal owned the rights to make a King Kong film in 1976, simply because the novelization and serialization of King Kong had become public domain. They could make their movie, but they didn't have exclusive trademark rights to the name. Judge Robert W. Sweet ruled in Nintendo's favor and when all was said and done, Nintendo was awarded $1.8 million for legal fees and lost revenue. Nintendo thanked John Kirby for winning the case by purchasing him a $30,000 sailboat named Donkey Kong. John Kirby would later have a character named after him - a cute pink ball known as Kirby.

With the success of Donkey Kong came sequels Donkey Kong Jr. In Donkey Kong Jr, Jr. had to rescue Sr. (Donkey Kong). from the evil Mario by climbing vines and avoiding "Snap Jaws." Donkey Kong 3 (DK3) took things in a whole other direction where you played as Stanley the Bugman - shooting bug spray at Kong while protecting your flowers from other bugs.

Donkey Kong wasn't the only success Nintendo was seeing the gaming business, though.

Gunpei Yokoi came up with a line of handheld gaming devices he called "Game and Watch". One day while traveling by train, he watched another passenger playing with an LCD calculator. His initial idea was a watch that had a game that you could play on the screen. These simple LCD units usually had a couple of buttons and were powered by watch batteries. With over 43 million sold worldwide, these glorified watches were a success. Nintendo produced these handheld consoles from 1980 to 1991, and they were the forerunners for both the Gameboy and Nintendo DS.

While Nintendo was seeing success in both the arcade and handheld gaming industry, the ground was beginning to crumble for the home console market.

Then 1983 came, the year that came to be known for the great video game crash. The console market had become oversaturated and was unable to sustain itself. Retailers were stuck with consoles and games that wouldn't sell, and seemingly overnight, the once thriving gaming market was gone. In 1985 Nintendo, decided to test the waters with its home gaming console in North America. In July 1983 the Famicom released in Japan and sold over 500,000 in two months. The Famicom would become known as the Nintendo Entertainment System. American retailers had not forgotten about the crash, only two years prior, so in order to sell the Nintendo Entertainment System (NES) in the test market stores, Nintendo offered to allow returns of all unsold units. This went against the wishes of Nintendo of Japan. All in-store setups and all marketing were created by NOA staff. It was a risky move, but if it worked Nintendo could grab almost all the market share in the home console business. Sega was releasing the Master System but didn't have nearly the marketing budget Nintendo did. After seeing success in all the test markets, Nintendo had a nationwide launch in 1986 and sold 1.1 million units.

From its beginnings as a Hanafuda card manufacturer, now Nintendo had become a household name with its home game console and new mascot, Super Mario. Kids across the nation couldn't get enough of Mario - he was everywhere. Mario cereal, toothbrushes, cartoons, and t-shirts. Mario had moved from a supporting role in Donkey Kong to the main attraction. The next chapter will tell the adventure of an Italian plumber who would become as big of an icon as Mickey Mouse.

Chapter 3: Mario's Adventure

From his humble beginnings as a carpenter trying to save his girl from his pet ape - to starring in over 200 games, Mario has been the face of Nintendo for over thirty years. The brainchild of Shigeru Miyamoto, Mario has done it all. He's saved princesses, raced go-karts and competed in the Olympics, but his story began on a construction site. He was the main character in a game that wasn't even named after him, and the sequel made him out to be the villain. That's like being the assistant to the regional manager. For Mario, it got worse before it got better, as he went from the construction site to a plumbing gig working in the sewers. Mario Bros hit the arcades in 1983, but it didn't have much success. It wasn't until two years later that we would see Mario again in Super Mario Bros on the Nintendo Entertainment System, and this time he would take us on an adventure, unlike anything we had seen before.

Side-scrolling games were nothing new, but nothing I played even came close to the adventures that Super Mario Bros offered. Thirty-two levels with different locations, some underground, some underwater, and some taking place at night. Each world had a castle and a dragon to defeat, and at the time it was nothing short of amazing! Here you are in this world full of enemies, traps, and few power-ups along the way. Magic Mushrooms that took you from ordinary to super. Fire Flower's that turned you "fiery" and the Starman that made you invincible for a short time. As a six-year-old kid in the mid-1980's, none of this seemed strange but thinking about this game getting pitched now makes me laugh. "So you play as this Italian Plumber from New York, and you eat mushrooms to become super. You're trying to save a princess from these turtles that have taken over her kingdom." No way this game could have come out any time other than the 80's, but I am so thankful it did. Here's the game description from the instruction manual (thankfully my mom never read it.)

One day the kingdom of the peaceful mushroom people was invaded by the Koopa, a tribe of turtles famous for their black magic. The quiet, peace-loving Mushroom People were turned into mere stones, bricks, and even field horse-hair plants, and the Mushroom Kingdom fell into ruin

The only one who can undo the magic spell on the Mushroom People and return them to their normal selves is the Princess Toadstool, the daughter of the Mushroom King. Unfortunately, she is presently in the hands of the great Koopa turtle king.

Mario, the hero of the story (maybe) hears about the Mushroom People's plight and sets out on a quest to free the Mushroom Princess from the evil Koopa and restore the fallen kingdom of the Mushroom People.

You are Mario! It's up to you to save the Mushroom People from the black magic of the Koopa!

Had my mom read that black magic was in the game it would have been "game over" before the game started. Black magic automatically put any game at the top of the unapproved list. Thankfully, I dodged a bullet there and was able to embark on this epic quest as Mario. Can we take a minute to pay our respects to all the Mushroom People that were killed due to the black magic turning them into bricks? I want to ask was the extra 50 points for smashing that brick worth the life of that Mushroom Person? At the time I was utterly unaware that Mario and I were causing the mass genocide of the Mushroom People! Knowing what I know now, I smash as few blocks as possible whenever I play. I'm kidding of course, but I was surprised to see how dark the story was. The story was one I couldn't wait to complete. I remember defeating Bowser for the first time and thinking I had done it only to hear Toad say, "Thanks, but your princess is in another castle." There was this mix of emotions inside of me: I was angry that I hadn't saved my princess, but I was stoked to continue the adventure.

It wasn't until years later that I could see how much the story and the game are like real life. Our goals are like the princess we try to rescue, but sometimes we come up short of our goal, and it ends up in "another castle". The remainder of this book will be looking at different aspects of the game, Super Mario Bros., and how to relate them to life, entrepreneurship, and enjoying the adventure.

Chapter 4: Enjoy The Journey

Remember back to Christmas part 4 1987, when my uncle told me to "enjoy the journey?" I didn't like hearing it, but I took it to heart, and I began to enjoy the journey with this Italian plumber. Now, thirty years later I'm still enjoying the journey to rescue Peach from Bowser, but I'm also enjoying the journey that this game put me on in life. My life has had plenty of ups and downs, and plenty of "another castle" moments. You know the moments, where you think you've finally succeeded, you've finally reached the top of the mountain you were climbing ... only to get a better view of the next mountain you need to summit. Sometimes in life we set goals, and we accomplish those goals, but there can be unforeseen consequences.

Let me give you an example; my senior year of high school I had one goal, and that was to get married. I worked on a dairy farm and hated every minute of it, but I was getting married and I needed to provide. Not having a career path as a goal has meant nothing but dead-end jobs for me my entire adult life. I never thought much about a career at a young age, other than being a youth pastor, which I landed a youth pastor job for two years and then that was it, I couldn't land another. My goal of marriage and family at such a young age has hindered me in the career department in a big way. That was my choice, but I had no idea the effect it would have on me long term. When I am at my lowest and haunted by regret, I ponder the "what ifs." What if I had chosen a career over family? The "what ifs" have zero benefits because they cannot change anything. The "what ifs" are like circling sharks while I am drowning in regret, and gratitude, is the life preserver I needed to stay afloat and move forward. My perception of me has always been that I am a failure. I zeroed in on the one aspect of my life that I wanted success in, my career, and was missing the best part of life, my amazing family. Depression was blinding me and causing me to regret the most important aspects of my life, my wife and kids. My perception needed an adjustment I had to let patience and gratitude take over. Once I realized that I didn't have to succeed immediately, I could enjoy the journey and love my wife and kids the way I was supposed to. The biggest lesson I learned here was the fact that I was blame shifting my circumstance instead of taking responsibility for them. My choices are what put me in this position and when I owned up to it, it allowed me to see that I have the ability to change it. The results will not be immediate (I will get into that later) and it allowed me to fall in love with the journey and in turn allowed me to find joy in the things that mattered, my family. I would be amiss not to mention Gary Vanyerchuk, it was insight on his podcast that helped me pull myself from the pit of depression and put me on the path of happiness and joy. I highly recommend checking him out if you share similar struggles. Speaking of my struggles, we still have more to look at.

I also carried around this limiting belief, from the time I was young, that I would never amount to anything. I'm not entirely sure where it came from. I was raised in a loving home, with supportive parents, but I have always had very low self-esteem. I always looked to the approval of others, which I believe led to a crippling fear of failure. I didn't set goals or have dreams because I assumed I they would be unattainable. I figured I couldn't let anyone down if I never tried, and if I never tried, I would never fail. What I was doing is the very definition of failure to me now. Never trying is failing. Lack of success isn't failing, it is part of the process of success. My mom used to ask me what my dreams were and I would tell her I had none so that I wouldn't be disappointed when they didn't happen. Sorry mom, I am sure that was hard to hear. By the age of twenty, we had our first kid and I worked multiple jobs to provide, so going to school wasn't really an option, and I had no idea how I'd pay for school anyway.

I bounced from job to job after working on the farm and settled on being a carpenter. Sadly I had no pet ape to rescue my girlfriend from. I've never enjoyed the work but it was there, so I learned the trade. I carry massive regret for not trying to get into a gaming career early on, but at that time I wasn't even sure what that looked like or where to look. Journalism never even crossed my mind, I thought I would never be a writer. I lived in the moment, and never really set any real goals. I played music, I played video games and worked dead-end jobs to provide for my beautiful little family. Throughout the years I have applied for better jobs, even had Microsoft seek me out only to offer the job to someone else. Even looking for jobs online leaves me feeling depressed and worthless, so I stopped. The reality is I won't be happy working for anyone but myself. Making it as a content creator is probably one of the hardest things to succeed at, but I'm enjoying the journey.

If your goal, like mine, is to make a living as a content creator, please understand that there is an element of luck involved. To make it in any business there's an element of luck. Also understand when I say luck I am not talking about having money fall out the sky into your lap. I am referring to opportunities that arise while you are working toward your goal. I want to make sure this is clear because believing that luck is the factor that is holding you back leaves room for excuses, and blame shifting. We don't have time for excuses and I'll touch on this more later. The entire reason for writing the second chapter was to showcase the luck that Nintendo had along the way. There are no guaranteed plans for success, you do the work, and hope that opportunity presents itself. Success cannot be forced, and if you put too much pressure on yourself and your business, you can miss the joy of the journey. I've been at this for over five years, and I've had a hard time celebrating small success, the "another castle" moments. These moments are the small breakthroughs when you finally reach one of your goals. You have to celebrate those moments. Sure your "princess" is in another castle, but look at what you just completed. I am horrible at this. I see the primary goal, I see the princess, and I carry the burden of being a failure because I haven't reached that goal. The primary goal doesn't happen without the small goals. The difficulty level in Super Mario Bros. ramps up with each level to better prepare you for what is coming, the same is true for your journey - each level better prepares you for the next. Completion of small goals along the way and celebrating them will help ease the burden of failure that you carry. The reality is you should never have picked up that burden, to begin with.

When you first played Super Mario Bros, or any game for that matter do you immediately tell yourself you are a failure cause you haven't beat it yet? Of course you don't. Starting a venture that takes time to grow doesn't automatically make you a failure because it hasn't succeeded. It needs time, just like you needed time to learn the levels and improve so you could proceed.

That last point may seem obvious because when you start out, it's exciting, but get three years in and you still hear that "your princess in another castle." It can wear on you and your mental health because you haven't reached your primary goal - you haven't reached your princess. You carry that burden, and it hinders you from enjoying the journey. Even as I write this, I think about the fantastic opportunities that have come my way, and I've taken little to no time to celebrate them. I've been working on celebrating more and recently my mental health has improved from celebrating the small victories. Your current life situation might suck, and whatever you're working on may be going slower than you like, but there's always good to be found. Look at the relationships gained or the knowledge that you have obtained. If you're in a creative endeavor look at what you have created, and celebrate it. Don't hate it because it hasn't taken off yet, it's still learning to fly.

 Maybe it's just life in general that has you down - look for the good. Spend time with loved ones, wrestle with your kids, play fetch with your dog, or lose yourself in a video game. There's beauty in the ordinary and mundane, in spite of everything you see on social media. So many people are living lives that seem so perfect. Did you start following them for motivation, but now you're envious? You get to see the best results from their journey daily on Instagram or Twitter, but rarely do you see the struggle. How often do people post who they really are? Stop comparing yourself to a post from someone that you see on your phone screen. If what once motivated you, now discourages you, remove it. Anything that is hindering your journey needs to go. Social media can be a fantastic tool as well as a tremendous time waster. Focus on the work you need to do - the next goal you need to reach to get to the next level. Turn your phone off and work. This princess isn't going to rescue herself.

One thing I hear a ton of content creators say is "I can do it better than them. Why are they so successful?" While you may be correct in your statement, thinking or saying it does nothing to help you. Celebrate the success of others. Be inspired by it, then get back to work. We live in a world of distractions, so you have to keep your eye on the prize. Better yet keep your eye on the small prizes, the small goals, and get after it. You know your end goal, but what is your yearly, monthly, weekly and daily goals? If you want to enjoy the journey, then set attainable goals, reach them, and add more if time allows.

When I first started with Super Mario Bros, the goal was to rescue the princess, but I couldn't even get past world 1-2. I couldn't get to the flagpole. I now had small goals to accomplish, and this goal would show up level after level in the form of a flagpole. I would get faster each time, successfully completing levels that used to end in a "game over" screen. I got to the point that I could use the warp pipes, but I would rarely go from world 1 to 4 because if I stopped in world 3, I could use the secret at the end of world 3-1 to get so many extra lives. A turtle is walking down the stairs and if you hit it just right Mario will continually jump on it rewarding you with many extra lives. You couldn't get too greedy though or the game would end on your next death. With all these extra lives, I was now prepared to take on whatever Bowser would throw at me. It was a process to get to that point, but now I could do it without losing a life. Every step of your journey is preparation for the next opportunity. Do you know how to measure progress in your venture? Growth isn't just the number of followers you gain or the number of views your content gets. Watching those numbers increase is great, but what if they stall out? Followers are not your progress meter - consistency is. If you want to know how to measure progress look to yourself. Have you grown? Have you learned? Measure your progress against your past self and celebrate that progress.

Your achievable goals shouldn't be numbers of followers or viewers, because that's outside of your control. And because it's out of your control, you can't beat yourself up for not achieving them. All of your goals should be goals you can reach yourself by working towards them. Writing five blog posts, or putting out three videos, or streaming for 20 hours. After those goals become the norm, you can then work on improving them. Can you add better photos to your blog posts or social media accounts, or could you improve your thumbnails on your Youtube videos or write better scripts? You're streaming 20 hours a week now, but how many highlights are you uploading to social media to showcase your unique content. Live streams are the hardest media for people to share, so give the world bite-size pieces of what they are missing when they don't show up. These are tangible goals based on the work you put in, not just left to chance. Now you can celebrate the fact that you are reaching goals and improving your content.

    I'll be honest, I hate the words followers or fans. I've always just felt that followers are people not just numbers, and I'd rather have friends than fans. Growing a community has been the best part of my journey. We chat daily in Discord **N64Josh.com/discord** (that link is an invite, and you're welcome to join), I love getting to know everyone and game with everyone. You never know how you can affect someone. I've had people say that they've never had anyone to talk about games with until jumping into the discord. Some have said that they've never had so many friends before and that's helped them cope with depression and loneliness. What was set up for a bunch of nerds to talk Nintendo games has become family. There are times that it's messy and people come and go, and that is just life. Set up a Discord or a Facebook group- someplace for your community to gather, to engage, and to be present. Don't use as it as a platform to only spam your content or products. Of course, you can promote, but don't only promote. Use it to connect, but be mindful of how much time you spend on it, because it can be very addictive and you still have work to do. Even writing this book I've had people tell me to "stop chatting in discord and get back to work." As the community slowly grows, you get to know the members, you become friends, and you get to game together. Growth will make getting to know people harder and harder to do, so enjoy it while you can.

My many hours with Super Mario were both frustrating and satisfying, and the same has been true for my many years of content creation. Learning to enjoy the journey has cut down on the frustration I experience significantly. Focus on what you've accomplished, set more goals to accomplish, and be ready whenever an opportunity comes your way. Let patience guide you. Anything worth doing takes time. Remember to enjoy the journey.

Chapter 5: The Side Hustle

Mario was a carpenter, and a plumber, who rescued princesses on the side. He stuck with that side hustle long enough, and eventually, he became the face of one of the biggest entertainment companies in the world. You may be in a situation where you pay your bills with a job you don't love. You know you want to do something you're passionate about, so decide what that is and get started. You can turn almost any passion into a side hustle, but you may need to get very creative. If a plumber can rescue princesses on the side, you got this. Choose something you are genuinely passionate about and build a community that you can add value to.

My first side hustle was photography. I started a blog and a podcast and thought I would be quitting my job within weeks of starting. I was shooting weddings, and things were going well. In fact, in one night my blog pulled in close to three hundred dollars in affiliate sales. I thought it was finally happening, but sadly, it wasn't. My passion fizzled, the jobs fizzled, I am still in the same position, and that venture has died. I love photography, but it wasn't what I was really passionate about. Gaming is what I wanted to cover, so I started a new website and podcast - n64gaming.com. I started this venture during the Nintendo WiiU era, and I was going to cover the Nintendo 64. The branding wasn't great and was even worse for the podcast. Most of the shows were interviews with indie game developers and I only occasionally talked about the N64. That's right, on the N64Gaming Podcast I interviewed indie developers. That poor branding was the result of not being able to come up with a name and just going with something - even though I didn't love it.

Then a game called Destiny came out, and I decided to cover that instead. TheLootCave.com was born and the Loot Cast, and it was all about Destiny until I was invited be a co-host of the Aim Assist Gaming Podcast which was also a Destiny Podcast. Long story short that venture also fizzled out.

When Nintendo announced the Switch, I was seeing a few podcasts popping up covering it, so I decided to do the same, and the Nintendo Power Cast was born. It is my most successful venture yet, and the last, and best, step I took was moving all of the branding to my name, N64Josh. I switched all my branding to N64Josh: Twitch, Youtube, Facebook, etc. All of those ventures in five year span and they had their ups and downs, believe me. Walking away from the Loot Cave branding was tough, and I wasn't able to just change names on Twitch I had to start over. Thankfully in less than a year, I've been able to catch up to and surpass the follower count of my previous channel.

Currently, my side hustle consists of weekly live streams on Twitch, recording at least 3 podcasts a week, reviewing games, writing blog posts and uploading videos to Youtube. It's a ton of work, but I love doing it. All areas of the brand are slowly growing each week, and small amounts of revenue are starting to trickle in from different sponsors and affiliate sales. The hub of all the content is N64Josh.com. If websites had been a thing in the 80's Mario would have started princessrescue.com, a site all about jumping over lava pits, kicking turtles, and outsmarting fire-breathing dragon. What's your side hustle, what is your passion?

First things first - you need branding and a recognizable logo. A mustache and blue overalls worked for our friend the plumber. My personal branding is a cartoon drawing of me holding a Nintendo Zapper and wearing a Nintendo Power Glove. My recommendation is that you brand yourself. That way you can change directions without having to start over. I have created multiple brands that now just sit in limbo because I couldn't find a way to pivot them. My personal brand (N64Josh) is now the umbrella for all of my other endeavors. Nintendo is proof that you can pivot a brand to different markets, but Nintendo as a name didn't tie it into one particular product. Go with a name that represents you, and, if possible, the audience you want to reach. Gamers are my target audience, and I've niched down further to Nintendo gamers because of N64. Nintendo has been my passion for 30 years, so creating content about Nintendo was a natural fit for me. Create a side hustle around your greatest passion.

Create content based on what you're the most passionate about. This will help you prevent burnout and keep you working at it the longest. I rarely play video games just for fun anymore. I am either streaming them and trying to be entertaining to my chat, or I am capturing footage for videos I need to make. What used to be a way to get away and relax is now work, but it's work I love. It is on me to make a point to play games for fun, and that helps fight the burnout, but when your job is to play, it's much harder to burn out. Playing for fun is getting some friends and just chilling out together or losing myself in a single player game. The same will be true for you, setting apart time to unwind is healthy. I have to force myself to stop work and enjoy my passion. This is hard for me because I want this side hustle to be my main gig, and I begin to feel guilty if I am not working on it every moment.

You also have to remember your loved ones. Work on managing your time wisely. Schedule family time, work time, side hustle time and play time and learn to be present for each one. Side hustle time and play time can bleed into each other, but there are times they need to be separated also. If you have a family of any kind, you need to schedule them in and be present. I'm talking about leaving your phone on the charger in your bedroom, so you're not looking at Twitter or Discord every two minutes. The support of your significant other is far easier to get when they know that they are not on the back burner. When it's their time with you, make it their time. Be diligent about making that time count. Come up with ideas that will make the time special. Netflix is ok some of the time, but come up with things that will create memories or something that will open the door for a conversation, like a puzzle or a board game. Being in the moment is the key. When it's time to work on the side hustle, it's a good idea to keep the phone away and focus on the task at hand.

    My current is schedule is crazy! I am up at 3:30 am Monday-Thursday working 4 am to 2 pm four days a week at my day job. I fire up my stream Monday-Thursday at 3 pm and stream for around 7 hours on Monday and Tuesday and Wednesday and Thursday I quit around 6 pm to spend time with family. Friday is pretty much an all day stream with couple of podcasts sprinkled in with family time that evening. I try to get bed by 10:30 or 11 during the week so coffee is my friend.

    Over the remainder of this chapter, I will give you a list of side hustles that you can do online, and they all relate to gaming. I will break down how I do each side hustle and what I have found that works, as well as the mistakes I have made. I do all four of these to help build my brand and grow the community I've built. I've had to teach myself to create websites, edit video, and use photoshop. And if I can do it, anyone can. Youtube will be your best friend if you want to learn something. I have learned as I go, so if I hit a roadblock, I would find the solution and keep on going.

Why four side hustles? The reason I recommend doing all four is because that is how I have seen growth. Some people get lucky, and all they have to do is one of these, and it works for them. That hasn't been the case for me. The four things I do every week are blog, stream, podcast, and upload to Youtube.

Blog

Your blog is the hub for all your content. This is where you can write news articles, game reviews, and post show notes for your podcast. This will give you one place you can send people to see all that you do online. Having a blog gives you the ability to rank in Google searches, and allows you to put out content that is easy to share. Shareable content is a huge part of building your brand, so put out the best quality content you can! Your website will have about seven seconds to get someone's attention before they bounce, so your content has to be clear, be concise and be what they are looking for. Use high-quality photos, and break your posts up into sections that clearly define what each part is about. You want someone that shows up to be able to quickly find what they are looking for. Rarely is someone going to read the entire article, most will just skim it so make sure you have something that will grab their attention.

    Wordpress is my blogging platform of choice. I use HostGator.com for hosting all my sites. You can easily install Wordpress and have a working blog in no time. (If you use code N64Josh you can save 25% at check out.) One of the biggest reasons I use Wordpress is all of the available plugins. My favorite plugin is called Pretty Link, which allows you to convert long, crazy affiliate links into manageable ones that can be said out loud on a podcast. Affiliate links are links to products that will enable you to make a commission if someone clicks them, and then purchases said product. Most of the time your affiliate link will be a very long link with many letters and numbers, but Pretty Link will spruce it up. I am an affiliate for The Beard Club, and the link is really long and ugly. I plugged that link into my Pretty Link plugin, and it's now N64Josh.com/beard. That link looks so much nicer than it did before.

    Becoming an affiliate is easy. If you have a product that you like, go to their website and scroll to the bottom of the page. Most of the time you will find the word affiliate or affiliate program. Click it and sign up. Amazon also has an affiliate program with commissions that are pretty low, but anytime someone asks for a link to something I give them an Amazon affiliate link. If they click that link I will make a commission on anything they purchase within twenty-four hours. I am fairly particular about the products I promote, so I will not promote something I don't use myself. The trust of my community is far more important to me than a dollar. Affiliate sales will be one of your revenue streams, and it's essential to have multiple revenue streams.

    Ad revenue from your blog is in another revenue stream, this will amount to very little at first because your site will need traffic to generate the income. All you have to do is sign up with Adsense, and they will automatically place ads on your site. They have tutorials on how to get set up, and it's relatively painless. You will also need an Adsense account to be able to run ads on your Youtube videos once your channel has one thousand subs and four thousand hours watched. Due to my rebranding, I started over with my Youtube channel and lost the ability to monetize my videos. I now use one of my sponsors to advertise in my videos. It's about a ten-second clip right at the beginning that showcases the gaming chair I use, and I mention my coupon code. Use tact with your advertising, because if you push too many products your audience may start to feel like a wallet. Keep in mind there's nothing wrong with giving your audience different ways to support you, but don't force anything.

Patreon.com is a way for you to crowdfund your content. There you can offer exclusive content and rewards for financial support. Get creative with the different tiers that you provide and overdeliver on each one of them.

Lastly, you could create your own product. One way is to self-publish a book, and also offer it as an audiobook give your audience more choices so they can consume the content how they like to. The website I use to self-publish is Gumroad.com. They are an affordable way to deliver products, and they allow me to have affiliates. Anyone can sign up and help me sell this book and make a small commission. Gumroad handles paying me as well as the affiliates. This saves me a ton of time. If you're already a content creator and want to become an affiliate, please email me: info@n64josh.com.

So far I've only touched on creating a blog for content creation. We still have podcasting, videos, and live streaming to cover.

Podcast

Podcasts are one of my favorite forms of media. You can find shows that cover topics that you're interested in, and as you listen to someone talk about issues you care about there's a connection that takes place. I've met other podcasters that I listen to and it feels like I already know them, and I've also had people tell me the same thing. It's a powerful medium and all it takes is passion, a microphone, and hosting. For hosting, I use podbean.com, and they have an unlimited plan for $14.99 a month. (My affiliate link for Podbean is **podbean.com/npc**) Once you upload the show to Podbean, they send it to iTunes, Google Play, Stitcher, Spotify and more. All you have to do is sign up with each of these outlets and submit your RSS feed that you can find in the settings dashboard on Podbean. Spotify is a little different, but you can apply to have you show on their service from the Podbean social tab. When you're first launching a podcast record a few practice episodes so you can figure out your format. What kind of segments do you plan on having? Will it be a solo show or will you chat with a friend? When deciding a name for the podcast, make it something that easily shows up in searches. I just started a Smash Bros Podcast and called it the Smash Bros Cast. Before starting the show, I did a search on iTunes and found no Smash Bros podcasts with Smash Bros in the title. Within days of starting the show, my new show ranks number one on iTunes when you search for Smash Bros. Pick a title that will allow for organic search traffic. The same is true for naming each episode. Don't title each episode with just a number. Title it with the topic of the episode so it can be found in searches. These few simple tips will help your show be found by listeners organically, and when you're starting out, you want as much help as you can get. When you first launch your show get five to ten episodes pre-recorded and upload them all at once. Hit up your friends and family to rate the show on iTunes. These two steps help your chances of getting on the new and noteworthy on iTunes, and that means more eyes on your new show.

You want to put out a quality show, so invest in a decent microphone. A Blue Yeti or Blue Snowball are both affordable options that will give you decent sounding audio. When you are recording, keep your mouth about an inch away from the mic, as the further away you get the more you sound like you're in a large room. Good mic control is essential and will give you a higher quality sound. You want to sound as pro as possible. I use a site called auphonic.com to level all my shows and take any hum out. They offer two hours a month for free and have paid plans for more.

Your podcast is also a tool to inform people of your other content. I've seen people show up to my Twitch streams that had found me through the podcast. I've had comments on Youtube videos from people saying they listen to my show. You want to be in as many places as possible, so people can find you and your content. As of writing this, I do three live podcast's a week, but each one also becomes a blog post and a Youtube video. Batch processing is your best friend. Double down on as much content as possible. Each one of my episodes has its own URL, example: n64josh.com/npc82 - that's the Pretty Link that I say during the show, so people can check the links mentioned. The content of the blog post includes the show notes I used for the episode, the audio and video version of the episode and all the links mentioned in the episode. I title the post the same as the audio podcast and the video. On both the video and the audio version, make sure to include the correct tags so you can improve your show's chances of be found organically through searches.

YouTube

Speaking of video let's talk Youtube. This is another excellent tool for you to utilize for brand recognition. Video creation is limited only by your creativity, so get creative. I feel like it's easy to look at creators that have large subscriber counts and try to mimic what they do, but the world doesn't need another one of them. It requires you. Being inspired by someone is great, but don't try to be them. Just because something works for them doesn't mean it will work for you. Look at them, be inspired and then do it better. Nintendo in the early years looked at what worked for the gaming companies before them, and then they did it better. What will set your videos apart from the ocean of noise that is Youtube? It's not as simple as just putting out "let's plays" and getting thousands of views. - For the record doing anything dangerous or life-threatening isn't what I'm talking about to set yourself apart. People have lost their lives over stupid stunts and views aren't worth it. - What are your strengths? Are you funny? Then make funny content. Are you good finding secrets in games? Then create tutorials. Videos that help solve a problem or teach something will usually have greater success on Youtube than opinion pieces talking over gameplay. Opinion videos have their place but they won't get you as much traction as a tutorial, or an article that clearly took research. Make quality content, don't just mail it in and hope for the best. Put out something you can be proud of. I've had some scripts for videos take me close to eight hours of writing and researching, and the video ends up being a half hour long. Your goal is putting out content that always leaves people wanting more. Remember how short people's attention spans are? Give them videos they want to watch until the end.

    Title your videos so they can be found in searches. I'll give you a quick rundown on keywords. If you ever hear the saying that something is "keyword rich," it means that it is full of the words that people use when they search for whatever subject the post, video or podcast is about. The Smash Bros Cast is keyword rich on iTunes because it ranks number one if someone searches for Smash Bros. There are tools that you can use to look up keywords and help you title your videos but as a general rule of thumb title your videos the same way people would search for them. Here is a basic example: as of writing this, I just reviewed a game called Skies of Fury DX on the Switch. I titled it Skies of Fury Switch Review, and it's the most-watched review video for that game at the moment. I left out "DX" in my title because I figured that most people would do the same when they searched for it. You can also use keywords to your advantage when using tags for your videos. If you want to see what's being searched, start typing what you think would be a good title and see what shows up first. That's your title, and that's where you'll find what your tags should be. Your tags don't need to be single words, they can be phrases that would be searched for, in the subject your video is about.

When it comes to getting video footage, you'll need a capture card. I use an Elgato HD60. A decent webcam, your smartphone or DSLR will work for getting video of yourself. Make sure to get a tripod of some kind, so your footage is smooth and not bouncing all over the place. If you use a webcam, you can use the Blue Yeti or Snow Ball, and your audio will be on point. For starting out, you can use iMovie on Mac or Windows Movie maker for editing. When you get the basics down, you can upgrade to something better. All of this takes time to learn, so set those small goals, and enjoy the journey.

Streaming

Live streaming is last but not least on the list. If you have the capture card, the mic, and the webcam, you're basically ready to rock. Having a decent computer also helps. You have three main choices right now: Twitch, Youtube and Mixer. My preference is Twitch only because it is where I started. Twitch has been around the longest and is also owned by Amazon. I stream on Twitch, but everything I go over in the next few paragraphs should carry over to all three. Streaming is some of the most fun I have had with content creation because interacting with my community in real time is like a virtual arcade. A bunch of nerds gathered for a common interest talking, laughing and sometimes working through the junk that life throws at us. I look at my community like family, they aren't just "fans" - I hate that word, remember? Hitting the button to go live and having twenty to thirty people show up is an incredible feeling, but it all starts with one. One person that is always there, that connects with you and gives you someone to talk to. When you start streaming, it can be mighty lonely. You can struggle with having an empty chat and trying to talk to yourself so that if someone does show up, they might come back. It will be challenging, so be ready for that.

When that one person starts showing up consistently and chats with you - the real fun begins. Please think about this for a second. There are a million other things that person could be doing, and they are spending their time with you. That is still crazy for me to think about. I went through months of just one person showing up, and then eventually two or three. Sometimes it was back to one but I stuck with it, I kept grinding and now usually there are over twenty people in chat. I went from streaming only one game to streaming a variety of games. I have learned that you need to stream what you enjoy, not what you think will help you grow. Take time to spend time in other creator's streams, be inspired.

While in those other's streams don't self-promote. Don't even mention your stream unless the streamer asks you about it. Network with your fellow streamers. Networking means building relationships with them, it does not mean using them as a stepping stone. Have the mindset of growing together. When you're networking, find out how your strengths may be able to help them and vice versa. You may be good at editing video, and they may be good at graphics. Use each other's strengths. Game with other streamers - do multi-streams and introduce each others audiences to each other. Don't look at them as competition. We are all stronger together.

Streaming has been the hardest part to grow, but also the most rewarding. One reason that it's tough to grow your stream is that it's not really shareable content. While you're streaming, you can make clips of your stream. You land a crazy kill, clip it. You crush someone's dreams at the finish line on Mario Kart, clip it. Each of those funny or amazing clips become thirty-second commercials for you to use on social media. Download the clips on to your phone, so that you can upload them to all the social media apps you use. Let people see what they are missing, and include your schedule or next scheduled stream in the post. Do you know the word that I said twice in that last sentence? Schedule. You need to have a schedule. My scheduled streams draw many more viewers than the sporadic ones. If people have the opportunity to plan for something, there's a higher chance they will show up.

I've heard so many successful streamers say that "consistency is key." You need to be streaming when you're scheduled to, but consistency alone isn't going to grow your stream. That's especially true with twenty-five thousand new streamers pressing that go live button for the first time every quarter. You have to market yourself, and podcasting and Youtube videos are a way for you to do that. Do a pre-show live stream with Twitter, Instagram or Facebook - answer a few questions and let them know the party will be live on your Twitch channel in ten minutes. Create short intro videos that you can use for your going live tweet. I created one that looks like an 80's or 90's sitcom intro. You're on a creative venture so get creative. Think about what you can do to make yourself stand apart from the rest. Remember to double down on your strengths - if you're funny then bring the jokes, if you're excellent at a particular game then bring the skills. My streams are about community and chilling out together, but that doesn't mean they can't change. It's ok to evolve and push yourself to improve. If you think about it, we are all like digital street performers playing our instruments with our cases open, hoping someone will throw us some change. We want to be the best, to draw the biggest crowd, so that our side hustle can become full-time.

    The goal is full time, but it can take years to reach. So enjoy the ride, work hard, and don't be disappointed when your princess in another castle. You're still making progress.

Chapter 6: Mushrooms and Fire Flowers

When I think about Mario going off to rescue Princess Toadstool, I think he could have made so many excuses for why it wouldn't work. He was short, and he was facing monsters that were the same size he was. Death was around every corner, and on top of that, there was all the running and jumping. I wonder if Mario was into CrossFit before it was popular? I guess jumping barrels while running through a construction site was good preparation for the Mushroom Kingdom. He was facing the unknown and getting ready to tackle it, head-on. There were a few power-ups to aid his journey, but it all boiled down to Mario trying to reach his princess.

With a controller in hand, our adventure began - World 1-1 - and like I said it didn't start out so well. Death after death, wanting to rescue the princess, but not being able to complete the first world. "This is too hard," or "it's not fair" would come out of my mouth. "If only I had better power-ups." Notice that each one of those statements pushes the blame to something I deemed out of my control; therefore, it was justified. I pressed on deeper into the game and eventually completed a level, then another level, and then a castle. My drive to finish was greater than the urge to quit.

All of this has been true in my creative endeavors. There are thousands of really good excuses you can make to quit, or never even start for that matter. Mushrooms, Fire Flowers and the occasional Starman, were all that Mario had. You may lack some of the tools you think you need to get started, but it's just an excuse.

I want you to take every reason that you have for quitting or not starting, and I want you to break them down. Look at the problem before you, and break it down into all the little issues that form the massive problem that you feel justifies an excuse. Maybe you don't have a computer, so you'll start when you get one. That excuse allows you to feel justified in waiting. But it's time to ask yourself, "What steps are you taking to get that computer?" You could get a part-time job working nights and weekends and save all that money towards your computer. Is working on the side not really an option? Put your smartphone to use.

You can download apps for Wordpress, Twitch, and Youtube. From your phone you can write a blog post, you can live stream, and you can edit and upload videos to YouTube. You are holding all the tools you need to get started in the palm of your hand. Will you be limited in what you can create? Sure, but putting out content and growing your brand now will always put you further along than waiting for the right gear. You can sit and wish for what could be, or you can get to work. It won't be easy, but nothing worth doing is.

I can promise you that the further you get into your creative endeavor, the more problems you will encounter. Super Mario Bros was the same way - the further you get into the game the difficulty ramps up, but you're prepared for it, and you move forward. As you encounter problems in your endeavor figuring them out and solving them will become easier. When I play Super Mario now, I run through every level not even needing power-ups, but that's only possible because of how many times I've played it. It's only possible because I didn't quit when it got too hard. Excuses not only rob you of so much, but they rob every person that you could've touched, entertained or inspired. Let that motivate you to take the tools you have and begin creating now. Shane Koyczan, put it best when he said: "there's a world dressed in shadows waiting for you to shine." Excuses keep your light from shining. It's time for you to come out from behind the curtain, and let your radiance be seen. You will trip, you will fall, but most importantly you will learn. Making excuses will rob you of what you could be learning. These excuses do not deserve the power bestowed on them.

There are two paths before you. One is a walk in the park that leads nowhere. The other isn't a path at all, rather you forge the way yourself with the tools and knowledge you have. Like reaching a new level in the game, you don't know what's before you, but you can know that there's joy in the adventure.

Chapter 7: Another Castle

"Thank You, Mario, but your princess is in another castle." That statement brought on a few different emotions for me when I was a kid. Confusion, because I thought I had finally reached the goal. The dragon had been defeated. What do you mean my princess is in another castle? As a seven-year-old kid, every story that involved a dragon ended when the dragon was defeated. But now I had to keep going? Do you know how hard it was to get to the end of 1-4 only to be informed that I wasn't the hero yet? That feeling of confusion has hit me at many points in my life, those moments where It looks like the stars are aligning and, I am finally going to succeed, only to hear "your princess is in another castle." One night, in particular, comes to mind.

Remember the photography blog I mentioned earlier and the evening I made about three hundred dollars from affiliate sales of an ebook? I set my phone to make the sound of Mario collecting a coin every time an email came in saying I had made another sale. It was amazing to hear the coin sound over and over again like Mario had found a block that was loaded with coins. I remember thinking that I had finally done it. I would be able to give my two weeks notice and start living the life that I had dreamed about. One day later the sales fizzled and what was the biggest high in my adventure thus far was now becoming the longest fall to my lowest point. I let my expectation get the best of me. Confusion, disappointment, frustration, anger, and depression were the next levels on my journey. The next product came out, and I only sold a fraction of what I sold before. I replicated everything I had done, but it didn't matter... it wasn't happening. With the next product, the same thing, only minimal sales. To be honest, it killed me inside that I wasn't able to replicate what had happened that night. That expectation is a double edge sword that has to be managed. You need to expect to succeed in your long-term goal and work towards it, but there's also a toxic expectation that you have to keep in check. Toxic expectations are the expectations that show up out of the blue when you experience success or failure.

My princess, my goal is self-employment, and I believed it was happening. I figured the next product would be more sales and the following even more sales, but that wasn't the case. I was still working a job I hated and didn't feel any closer to my goal. My princess was in another castle, and I had to deal with that. I didn't handle it well, and to this day I still struggle, but I have been able to attack those feelings of confusion, disappointment, frustration, anger, and depression. The root of every one of those emotions and feelings, in my case, was a toxic expectation. There are times that expectation is apparent - my sales blew up one day, and I expected it to happen again. It was like watching a 1up Mushroom coming right at me, and then fall into a pit before I could reach it. That 1up Mushroom could prolong the adventure and help me achieve the next level. All those sales coming in, the sound of Mario collecting coins become nothing more than an echo, and I was crushed. What I thought was the end of one chapter, and the beginning of a new one turned out to be the same chapter. It was like someone hitting the reset button while I was in the middle of the game. My toxic expectations of continued success were the result of the small success I had seen that night, and when my toxic expectation wasn't met, it opened the door for disappointment, frustration, depression, etc.

With the door open, they came in like uninvited guests that had nowhere else to go. Words cannot express how detrimental the unwanted guests can be, and they needed to be shown the exit. I needed to remodel this door to be a revolving door that unwelcome guest can exit through as quickly as they entered. These uninvited guests breed all kinds of negative feelings that will kill your motivation, feed entitlement, and put unnecessary stress on the venture and your relationships.

When the sales stopped coming in, do you have any idea what it did to my motivation? It killed it. I had taken my eyes off the primary goal and now focused on the new shinier goal, and when it failed, I looked at myself as a failure. I found myself asking questions like, "What's the point?" Looking back, the simple answer is the same answer it has always been and always will be; the point is the goal -the princess. In the moment of frustration and disappointment that answer is far less clear. In fact, the only clear answer at the time was that I was still a failure because I could not reproduce what happened that night all the sales came in. Because of toxic expectations, I was now wearing the title of failure, and each time another book came out, and I didn't see more sales, that point was driven home. The goal shifted from building a community to making sales, and neither was happening, and I was depressed and unmotivated.

Depression was taking a toll on everyone in my life, my wife could see me hurting and helped carry that burden, but that weight wasn't fair for me to put on her. At work, I was like an exposed nerve that was frustrated and angry. I didn't want to talk to anyone there - I didn't want to be there, and my hope of leaving had vanished. I was miserable and didn't really care if it affected the people around me. Looking at it now I see how selfish it is, but that's why hindsight makes everything so clear. I would continually tell myself that "it wasn't fair" as if I deserved it. That's clear evidence of entitlement, and it is an incredibly dangerous mindset to have. Self-pity may soothe your wounds for a moment, but it's a cancerous solution that will have long-term negative effects. If "it's not fair" then why do you even keep working at it? It's an excuse that will hold you like a crutch when you wonder why you aren't reaching your goal. The entire time I was dealing with the depression, I knew it was self-inflicted, but I had no clue how to get out of it. I don't believe that is the case for everyone, but it was for me. What was supposed to be an exciting adventure, working toward my dream, was now the source of my pain and frustration. The toxic expectation had walked through the door of my mind, and I didn't know how to get it to leave.

 I want you to set up the revolving door in your mind so that whether success or failure comes your way you do not let it deter you from your primary goal. I want you to meet the houseguests that will help you find happiness; Patience and Gratitude. Start this adventure knowing it could take seven to ten years to take off. Are you ready to work that hard and that long?

 Be grateful for the air in your lungs. Be thankful for the fact that you are starting a side hustle in a time that has more opportunities than any before it. Another castle moments don't need to be monumental moments that make or break us. Celebrate the fact that you have cleared a stage, and then get back to work on the next one. Enjoy the moment and start the next level. It's important to celebrate the successes because it's proof of progress, but celebrate without inviting toxic expectation in, and if he does come in show him the exit.

The toxic expectation is relentless just like Bowser at the end of each world, and you need to attack it head-on. Whenever I finished a world in Super Mario Bros I didn't have a massive celebration, it was more like a mental pat on the back, and I got back to it. The princess still needs to be saved - I needed to get back to work. At the same time, I didn't throw a pity party because my princess wasn't in this castle, I just kept on going. The point I want you to take away from this is that each time you accomplish a small goal or fail at a small goal, acknowledge it, learn from it, and get back to work.

When it comes to expectation, expect to work, and work harder than you ever have. Plan to fail, prepare to learn. Don't expect instant success, don't expect the luck someone else has had to happen to you. Don't expect this to be easy, because anything worth doing never is.

Chapter 8: Only Moving Forward

There's only one direction in Super Mario Bros, and it's forward. The same is true with life - it just moves forward. If you miss a mushroom in the game you can't go back for it. Do you stop playing? No, you adapt, you move forward, maybe a little more carefully, but you move forward. Moving forward is all you have. Looking back and asking "what if?" will only hinder your progress. The next time you play Super Mario Bros try going backward after you've gone forward. You hit a wall and go nowhere. I cannot stress to you enough the importance of moving forward. When you dwell on the past or what could have been, you will hit a wall. Let go of the past and move forward.

The voice that you have in your head that loves to feed negativity and beat you down is the same voice that will feed the idea that "things could have been better if…" Hindsight is great, and maybe things could have turned out different, but you will never know so keep going forward. When you look back at your life, you will see clearly the choices you made that have placed you at this moment. "What if this?" And "what if that?" will not change the present. Looking back is easy since you can see who to point the finger at for your current situation. Dads seem to be the most natural target or maybe a teacher in school.

It does not matter who you point the finger at, because it will not change anything. Playing the victim will not change your current circumstance. You may be entirely justified in pointing the finger at someone for your current situation, but it will not improve your situation. Looking back on what could have been is a colossal waste of time and will destroy your motivation to move forward. It can be easy to wallow in self-pity, and it can feel good to point the finger because it allows you to blame your current situation or lack of success on someone else.

You may be saying to yourself, "but my situation is unique, you've never walked in my shoes." You are correct, I have not walked in your shoes, but I have walked in self-pity, or better put, I've sat stagnate in self-pity looking back instead of moving forward. By no means am I downplaying any hurt you are allowed to feel, but I want you to be able to move forward. If possible, forgive. It will do wonders for your mental health. Forgive, not only others but yourself. I pile on the blame like blankets of regret and the voice in my head has a hay-day with it continually reminding me that I am wasting my time and will never succeed.

Regret is like that Koopa Shell you kick into a wall, and it immediately comes back and takes you out - it's vicious. Eventually, you learn to jump over the shell as it comes back to you and you continue onward. When your regret is continually thrown back in your face you do not have to let it stop you from moving forward. Instead, let progress be your momentum and keep going just like Mario, jumping over the shell. Do you remember the turtles I mentioned in chapter 4, the ones in world 3-1 that are walking down the stairs and you can get all the extra lives you need? Those extra lives are the result of kicking a shell into a wall over and over again, and the extra lives mean more progress in the game. Kicking the shell into the wall just went from bad decision to an amazing one, and regret is no different. Your regret doesn't have to hinder your progress and instead can be used to help others on their journey as well. Regret would love to see you stagnant, but I say flip it on its head and use it to help others. Where regrets exist, there is also something to be learned and something learned can be taught. Pass the knowledge you have gained from your past experiences to the less experienced. Help them to avoid the same mistakes you made, and the next time the voice in your head brings up your past you can come up with a way to help someone else's future.

    Every Monday morning I get to my job, and the voice in my head reminds that I still haven't made it and probably never will. Some mornings I believe it, and it throws my entire day off, but recently, it has not been the case. I have been getting up early and working harder than ever before. I silence the voice by moving forward. As a kid playing Super Mario Bros, I hated missing the power-ups, but I kept moving forward. I didn't dwell on the missed Super Mushroom, I continued on.

You need to move forward. Even if it's baby steps you need to move forward. What can you do now that will move you closer to your goal? If your goal is to write a book, start a with a sentence a day. If there's something you want to create, start now and do it daily. You want a better job, then you better get started on the new resume or start learning the skills you will need for that new position. Every step forward no matter how small will help silence that voice that says "you can't and won't." You are more than what the voice in your head tells you that you are. You can prove that voice wrong by moving forward and striving for your goals.

Chapter 9: Hitting Reset

In world 1-2, near the end of the stage, there's a glitch that allows you to enter the negative stage. It is a stage that has no end, and you swim and swim until you reach the pipe, and then you start the level over. You have to hit the reset button once you enter this level or wait until all your lives are depleted and start over.

There will be times in your adventure that you are putting the work in, but you feel like you aren't getting anywhere. You may have to hit the reset button. Coming to this conclusion does not happen overnight. I have hit the reset button on some ventures, and it has been difficult every time. I worked on a photography blog for almost two years, but near the end, I really didn't enjoy it any longer. I never felt like I was connecting with anyone in that community. Remember the podcast I mentioned earlier The Loot Cast? It was all about Destiny, and when the sequel released and the launch was less than spectacular, I pulled the plug on that show. One hundred and twenty-eight episodes and I called it quits. A part of me hates that I couldn't make that show a success, but I learned so much about podcasting and content creation that learning was the success. When I pulled the plug on that show, I had already begun a Nintendo podcast that was seeing far greater success. It made sense to put more time and energy into the new podcast. Shutting down the Destiny show didn't just happen without me trying new ideas and pivoting, but nothing I was doing was working.

As a kid, I would attempt the negative world from time to time trying to find the end, but every time it ended with the same result - frustration. I would try to swim backward or check the pits to see if there was a secret I was missing. Maybe I could swim as fast as possible and reach the end before a certain time? But I kept getting the same result each time. This can happen in your venture as well.

You get to a point where you feel like you have exhausted every avenue, but you are no closer to your goal. It's one thing to work at something for a month and not see much return; it's another thing to work at it for years and not see much of a return on investment. If after your first month you are frustrated with the lack of growth, you may need to reevaluate your expectations. If years have passed and everything you have tried hasn't helped you progress to the next level, you may have to hit the reset button. Does that mean you have failed? Absolutely not. You take note of everything you learned and start again.

My goal, my rescued princess, is having my own business. Every time I have hit the reset button, it's been after I have started something else that was seeing greater success, in less time. I modified my path with my passions. My passion for Destiny was gone and I didn't enjoy the game, so talking about it week after week became a chore. I watched the download numbers grow smaller and smaller because people could tell the passion was gone. Nintendo is where my love is. When I would stream, write news articles, and record podcasts about Nintendo, it didn't feel like work at all. The joy of creating Nintendo content is evident in the product.

You know what your ultimate goal is. Now you need to find the path that will help you reach that goal. If the road you are on isn't helping you progress, then hit the reset button and begin forging a new path. I am not saying throw in the towel and quit. What I am saying is this - if your original path has stalled out find a new one. Be mindful of your progress. Are the daily goals you are setting helping you grow or have they stalled your progress? If your venture has you in a place where you do the same thing week in and week out, but you don't experience growth it's time to mix it up.

It takes more than consistency to grow a business. Consistency is one of the critical ingredients for sure, but so is creativity. You are on a creative endeavor, so get creative with how you will grow your brand. I recently mixed it up with my Monday night streams, and instead of just streaming Mario Kart, I am now interviewing my community members while we race. The first week I started this, the number of viewers doubled from the previous week. Had I stayed on the path of only streaming without the interviews on Mondays, I may have burned out. But before hitting the reset button, I mixed it up. I noticed that all the streams that are talk shows would pull double the numbers of the non-talk shows, so why not add another talk show? Now my live stream on Monday has a greater pull than before and each interview becomes a YouTube video.

Look at the strengths of your brand, what you are doing well, and double down on them. Take a look at your content, and ask what is gaining the most traction? Whatever it is, do more of that. Mindlessly grinding day after day with little to no results is a path to burnout. If you are stuck in the negative world, hit the reset button. Forge a way that is fueled by passion and creativity. Watch for signs of burnout and rely on your strengths to keep the content fresh and enjoyable for you to do.

Hitting the reset button shouldn't be something you take lightly. I look at it as a last resort when you know that it's time to move on. No one can tell you what that looks like or how that feels. With The Loot Cast, I set a goal for a couple of months after the game released. If it didn't hit the numbers I was aiming for, and the game was failing, I would call it quits. The numbers didn't increase even after adding co-hosts and trying new things, so I called it quits. I felt like I did my best and after two and a half years it was time to put energy elsewhere.

I can look at it now and see all the ways I could have done it better because I am doing it better with my current shows. I am more organized now, and nothing is thrown together. I am continually looking for ways to add value to my listeners. Podcasts are a way for people to be informed while they are working out or driving, so the value I want to give them is information. What games are on sale, what games are releasing this week, and what is going on in the world of Nintendo? Those are the questions I aim to answer each week, to save my listeners time from having to look that up in their free time.

Before you hit the reset button ask yourself, "How can I add value to those that find my content?" Come at that question from many angles and if you're struggling to answer it, look to others that do what you do and are succeeding. Take inspiration from them. How can you improve upon what they are doing? The fastest way to get people to like your content and share your content is to add value to them. So make that happen. Adding value and keeping your passion alive will keep your finger from pressing the reset button. Work hard, persevere when things get tough, and keep your finger on the pulse of what you are doing to avoid getting stagnate or burning out and having to hit the reset button.

Chapter 10: Player 2

I spent many Saturday mornings waking up early at my buddy's house, and we would tiptoe downstairs to the living room. Grabbing the Super Mario Bros cart and inserting it into the NES - but not before blowing on it first. We would fire up the system and stare at the opening screen. It was a joy to press the select button and begin this adventure with my best friend. Of course, I made him play as Luigi, like I said earlier, cause that's how I roll. I have so many memories of playing together, reaching new levels, and celebrating accomplishments.

Having a player 2 in life is so very important because you don't want to go through this alone. My main player 2 is my wife. She's my best friend and as of recent my main real-life friend. Having her support is so needed when I am down, and having her to celebrate the wins with is huge for me! If I didn't have her, I wouldn't really have anyone that I could talk to in person. I have focused so much on the side hustle, that I have neglected friendships and community with people around me. My online community is fantastic, and I wouldn't trade it for the world, but it's important to have friends in real life also.

Having that drive to achieve your goals is great, but not at the expense of giving up relationships. My head is down, and I work every day before the sun rises and after it sets. I feel guilty when I am not working, and that is part of the reason that I stopped hanging out with people. I only have so much time in the day and don't want to waste any of it. Let me make something very clear, having human contact and spending time with people over coffee, or a meal is good for you. Getting to this point wasn't a decision I made one day, it just happened over time. I became too busy with everything that wasn't work or family, and I'm now lonely because of it. I don't want to see anyone end up in this same situation, so please schedule time with friends into your busy life, because it's worth it. In my mind, I tell myself that I will have more time for friends once my business is off the ground and I can quit my day job, but will those same people still be there? Success does take sacrifice, but friendship doesn't belong on that altar. Set up a coffee date with someone now. When it comes to friendship, finding like-minded people can be tough. That is a factor in why a lot of my friendships have fizzled out. Most of my old friends and I have very little in common any more, but that's not an excuse to give up on friendship. I may need to get out of the house more and find local gaming tournaments to meet some people with similar interests. Finding and making new friends is not only good for you but can be good for them as well. You have something to offer in the friendship, so get out there and make some friends.

Building a community and having online and long distance friends are still critical. I meant it when I said I wouldn't trade it for the world. There is a genuine connection with the people in my community. Conversations about depression or daily struggles happen in my discord, and I love seeing it because I know so many people feel alone and unable to share that with anyone. From that community, I have had people collaborate with me or even become a co-host on my podcast. Eric, the co-host of the Nintendo Power Cast, and I became friends over Xbox Live, and we have kept in touch for over 15 years. We have walked through some tough times together, and the relationship has had ups and downs, but we have worked through them, and he's one of my best friends.

The same is true for Mel, Bryan, and Mike. They are there to let me blow off steam when I need to vent. Content creation can be lonely so find other creators to befriend and talk through the ups and downs with.

Find your player 2.

Chapter 11: The Final Boss

I stepped away from this book for a few months and had been applying the advice I have written. Finding joy in the journey has become part of my primary goal. I know that I am writing my story and it is full of ups and downs and I am using gratitude and patience as my fuel. My goal of self-employment and doing something I love hasn't changed - that's my final boss for this part of the journey. It's the princess that Bowser has captured, and I will continue leveling up to slay that dragon.

Every four levels you fight Bowser again and just when you think you have finally got him figured out, he changes his tactics. The fire that he breathed was easy enough to jump over, but now he also throws a barrage of hammers at you making jumping more difficult. This is life in a nutshell. Just when you think you have it figured out, the next obstacle shows up, and that excites me. In my current state, I want to take on whatever comes my way. I will have days that I will feel beat down and like I am wasting my time, and in those moments I have to look at what I have done so far and see how far I have come. I will attack whatever life brings me, fueled by gratitude. That gratitude comes from the very fact that I am able to attack these obstacles. Each time I find out that the princess is in another castle, I will evaluate the situation and get to work. You have to do the same because complaining about it brings zero progress. You have no time to waste complaining, so don't do it. Don't go to Twitter and complain about your lack of growth, instead go to your player 2 and talk to them. Blow off some steam and get back to work. I am not saying you can't be frustrated from time to time but get out of that state of mind as quickly as you can. Combat complaining with gratitude and patience.

Your patience is key to your success more than anything else. The side hustle isn't a sprint, it's a marathon, and you need to know that going into it. Patience will allow you to enjoy the journey because it will remove the pressure of needing to succeed now. Are you ready to work at this for years? That is the mindset you need going into this. I am on my sixth year trying to build a business online, and this is the first time in that six-year journey that I am giving it the time it needs. This cannot be rushed, it is just like game development - it needs the time it needs. Plan on six to ten years to get your brand off the ground. If it happens sooner, it's like hitting that warp zone but don't expect it. Managing your expectations is crucial, and patience is the key.

My unrealistic expectations of the side hustle had a stranglehold on my joy. My depression was at an all-time high, and I was in a dark place. I was blind to what I had accomplished, and how my brand was growing. Patience and gratitude came in like a Super Mushroom and a Fire Flower, and I felt like I could take on anything no matter how long it takes. They helped me clear my head and celebrate what I have done up until this point. Am I where I want to be? No, but I'll get there eventually. You will get there eventually too if you're willing to put in the work and the time needed to get there.

    The journey will be full of ups and downs, failures and success, and this is true for everyone. The road to success is paved with failure - it is the by-product of trying to build something from nothing. Failing while trying is not actually a failure at all, it's learning. Keep learning and keep growing, and get that princess. Find joy every time you hear that your Princess is in another castle because you are that much closer to your goal.

Made in the USA
Monee, IL
04 May 2020